Jenny Ackland

At Home With
LETTER FORMS

OXFORD
UNIVERSITY PRESS

Introduction

The *At Home With* workbooks introduce and reinforce key numeracy and literacy concepts for primary school children. They provide lots of opportunities to develop the key skills that are the basis of primary school curriculum work. The workbooks are available in three levels: 3–5 years, 5–7 years, and 7–9 years. The activities are fun and are designed to stimulate discussion, as well as practical skills. Some children will be able to complete the activities alone, after initial discussion; others may benefit from adult support throughout. All children will enjoy rewarding themselves with a sticker when they reach the end of an activity.

Using the book

At Home With Letter Forms offers a variety of activities which focus, in particular, on the following:

- hand–eye coordination skills
- the formation of round letters, starting with a movement to the left
- vowels, their shape and sound
- the formation of letters with an initial downward stroke
- the formation of letters with an initial downward stroke, then up again, leading into a curved movement
- the formation of letters with a sharp point.

Many of the letters are grouped in families (letters of similar shape). As each new letter is introduced, encourage children to trace the letter with their finger, say the letter, say the sound it makes and then think of words that begin with this sound.

Not all the letters of the alphabet are introduced in detail in this book, although they all appear on pages 30 to 31. Refer to *At Home With Writing* for activities with more letters.

Oxford University Press
Great Clarendon Street, Oxford OX2 6DP

Oxford University Press is a department of the University of Oxford.
It furthers the University's objective of excellence in research, scholarship, and education by publishing worldwide in
Oxford   New York   Auckland   Cape Town   Dar es Salaam   Hong Kong   Karachi
Kuala Lumpur   Madrid   Melbourne   Mexico City   Nairobi   New Delhi
Shanghai   Taipei   Toronto

With offices in
Argentina   Austria   Brazil   Chile   Czech Republic   France   Greece   Guatemala
Hungary   Italy   Japan   Poland   Portugal   Singapore   South Korea   Switzerland
Thailand   Turkey   Ukraine   Vietnam

Oxford is a registered trade mark of © Oxford University Press
in the UK and in certain other countries

© Jenny Ackland 2006
The moral rights of the author have been asserted
Database right Oxford University Press (maker)
First published 2006
Reissued 2009
This edition 2012

All rights reserved. No part of this publication may be reproduced, stored in a retrieval system, or transmitted, in any means, without the prior permission in writing of Oxford University Press, or as expressly permitted by law, or under terms agreed with the appropriate reprographics rights organization. Enquiries concerning reproduction outside the scope of the above should be sent to the Rights Department, Oxford University Press, at the address above

You must not circulate this book in any other binding or cover and you must impose this same condition on any acquirer
British Library Cataloguing in Publication Data
Data available

ISBN: 978 0 19 273329 0

3 5 7 9 10 8 6 4 2

Designed by Red Face Design
Illustrations by Helen Prole, Mark Brierely and Oxprint
Printed in China.

Paper used in the production of this book is a natural, recyclable product made from wood grown in sustainable forests. The manufacturing process conforms to the environmental regulations of the country of origin

Contents

- Drawing circles 4
- Straight and curved lines 5
- Circles and lines 6
- The letters c and o 7
- The letter a 8
- The letters o, a, and d 9
- The letters c, g, and d 10
- The letter s 11
- The letters c, a, d, and s 12
- The letter e 13
- The letter e 14
- Vowels: a, e, i, o, u 15
- Vowels: a, e, i, o, u 16
- Vowels: a, e, i, o, u 17
- On or under? 18
- The letters r and n 19
- The letters r, n, and m 20
- The letters h and m 21
- The letter p 22
- The letters p and b 23
- The letters l and t 24
- The letters l and t 25
- The letters j, u, and y 26
- The letters v and w 27
- The letter f 28
- The letter k 29
- The alphabet 30
- The alphabet 31
- Summary of skills 32

Drawing circles

Draw round glasses on each face.
Colour the hair.

Straight and curved lines

Join the dots.
Colour one leaf and three fish.

Circles and lines

Join the dots.
Colour five spiders and one butterfly.

The letters c and o

Write the letters **c** and **o**. Say the sounds.

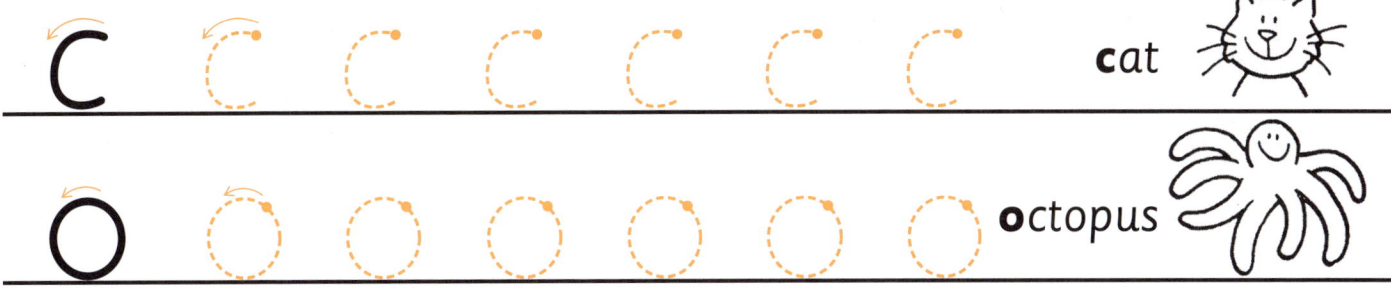

c c c c c c c **c**at

o o o o o o o **o**ctopus

Colour the **o** shapes.

The letter a

Write the letter **a**. Say the sound.

a a a a a a a **a**pple

Colour all the things that begin with **a**.

The letters o, a, and d

Write the letters **o**, **a** and **d**. Say the sounds.

o o o o   **o**range

a a a a   **a**pple

d d d d   **d**og

Write the first sound in each box.
Colour the things beginning with **d**.

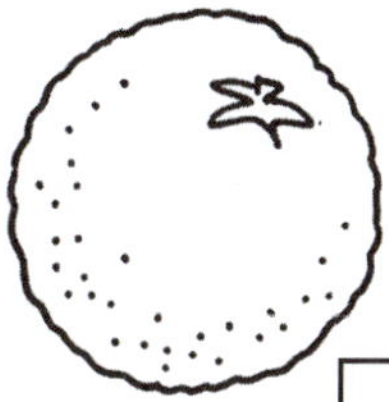

The letters c, g, and d

Write the letters and say the sounds.

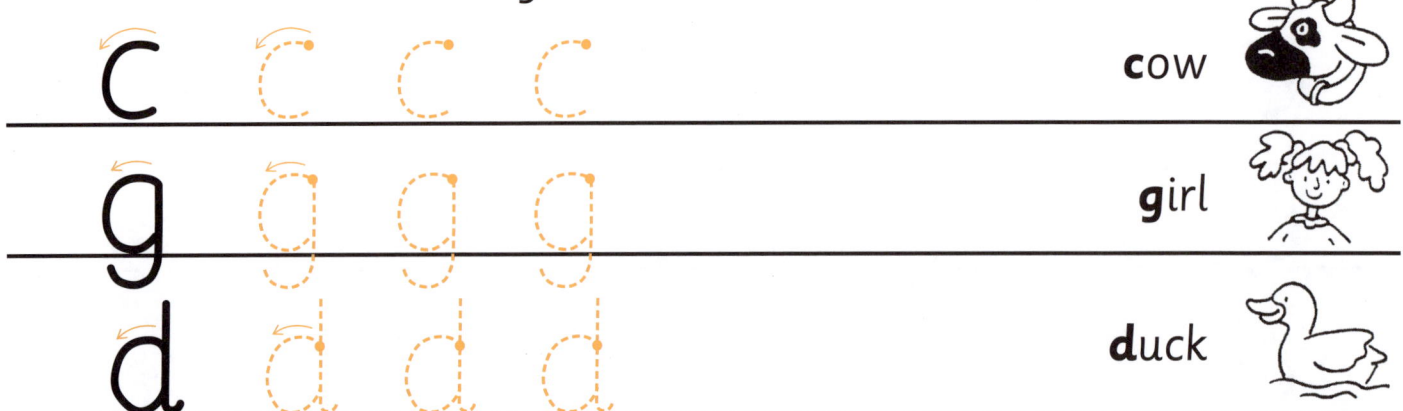

c c c c **c**ow

g g g g **g**irl

d d d d **d**uck

Write the first sound in each box.
Colour the things that begin with **g**.

The letter s

Write the letter **s** and say the sound.

s s s s   **s**ix 6

Write the letter **s** in each box and say the words.

The letters c, a, d, and s

Write the letters and say the sounds.

c c c c **c**at

a a a a **a**xe

d d d d **d**oor

s s s s **s**ix

Write the first sound in each box.

The letter e

Write the letter **e** and say the sound.

e e e e e e e **e**gg

Write e under the things that begin with **e**.

The letter e

Colour the things that begin with **e**.

Vowels: a, e, i, o, u

Write the letters and say the sounds.

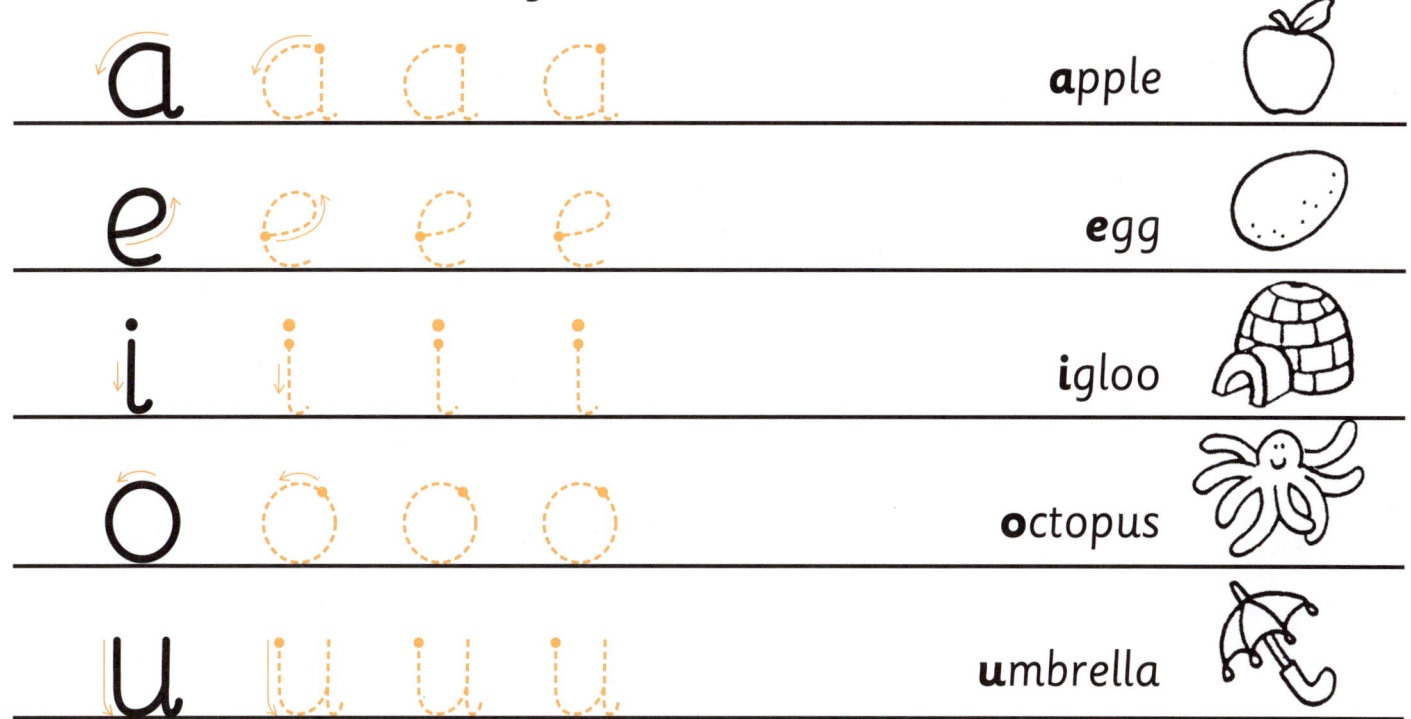

a a a a a   **a**pple

e e e e e   **e**gg

i i i i i   **i**gloo

o o o o o   **o**ctopus

u u u u u   **u**mbrella

Join the dots.

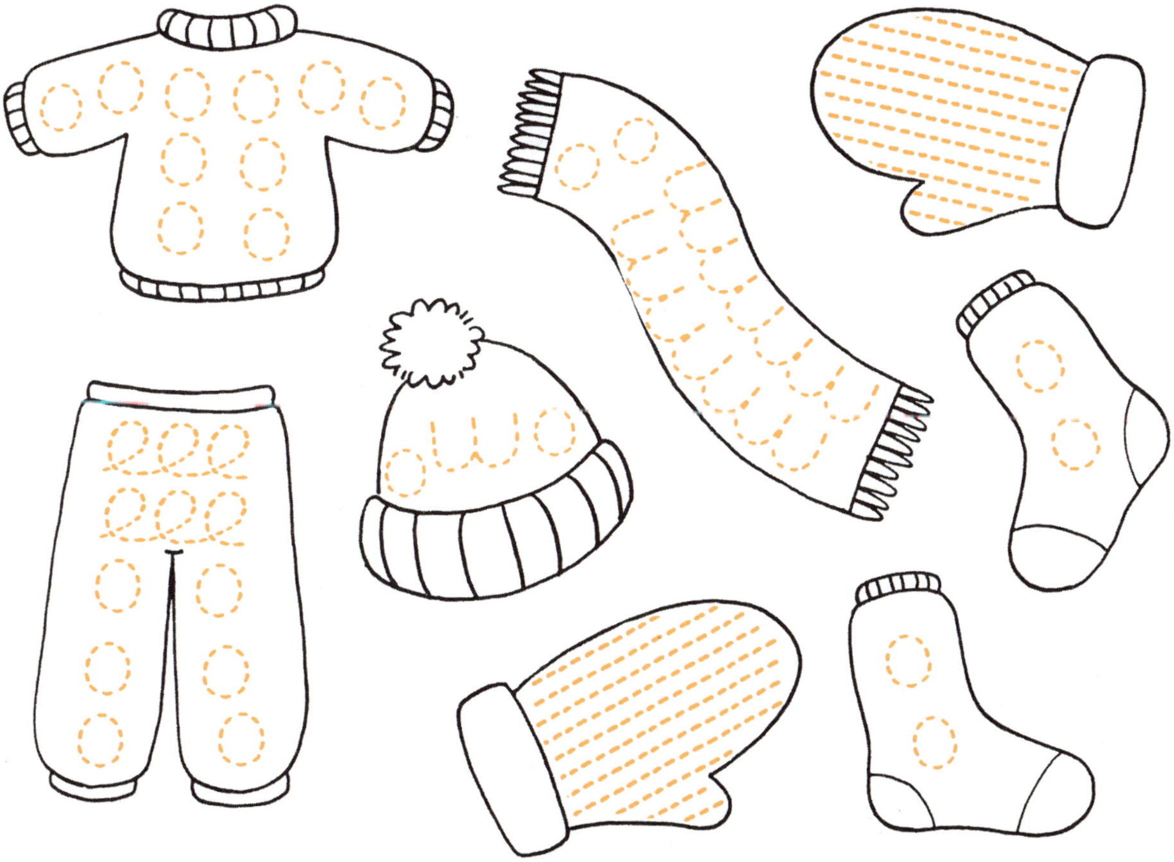

Vowels: a, e, i, o, u

Colour the pictures that begin with each letter.

Vowels: a, e, i, o, u

Write the letters and say the sounds.

a a a   o o o

e e e   u u u

i i i

Circle the letters that these words begin with.

f n g
m t (e)

p l s
u t n

s a e
d o m

u b g
p a r

a i h
d e r

b e l
c o s

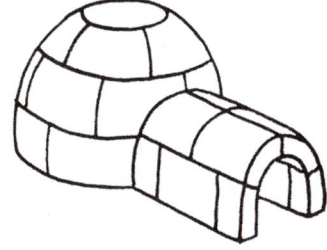

f j n
u i e

t m o
d c p

On or under?

Write **o** in the box for 'on'.
Write **u** in the box for 'under'.
Colour four pictures.

The letters r and n

Write the letters and say the sounds.

r r r r r r r r **r**ope

n n n n n n n n **n**ut

Write the first sound in each box.
Colour six pictures.

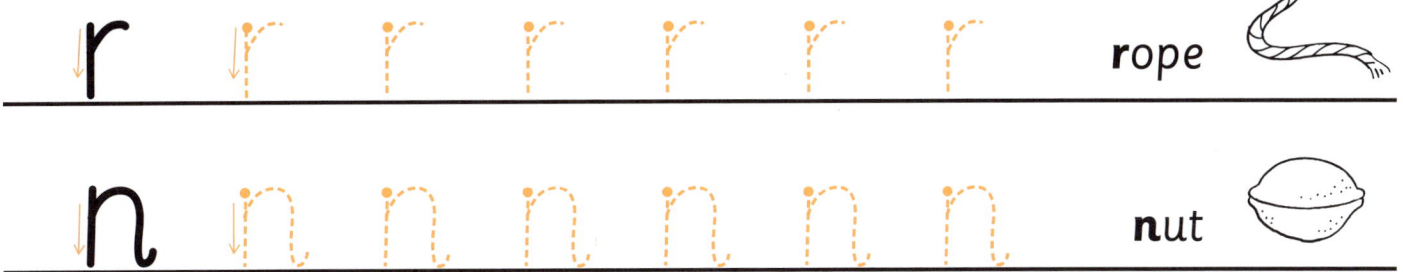

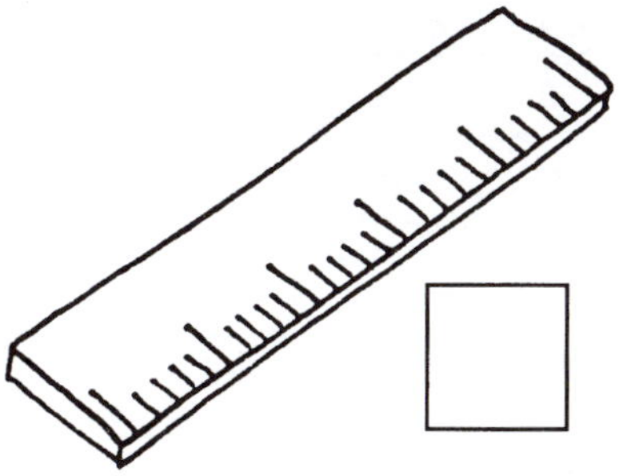

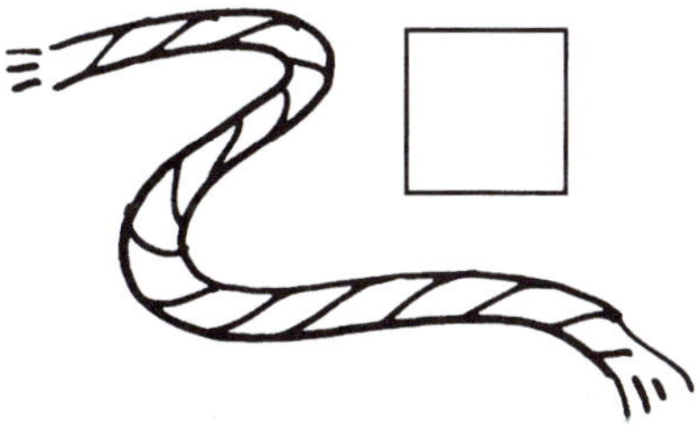

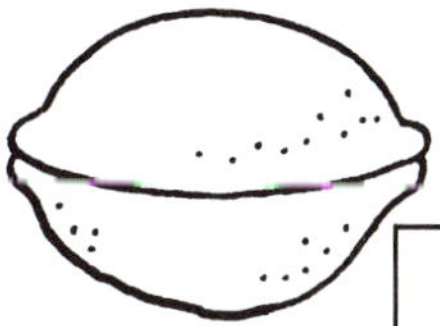

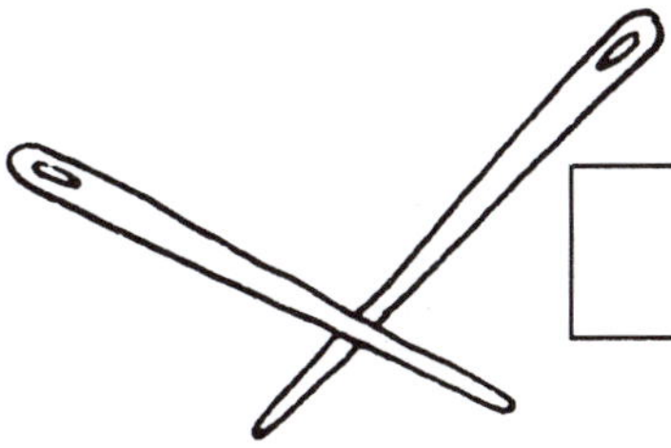

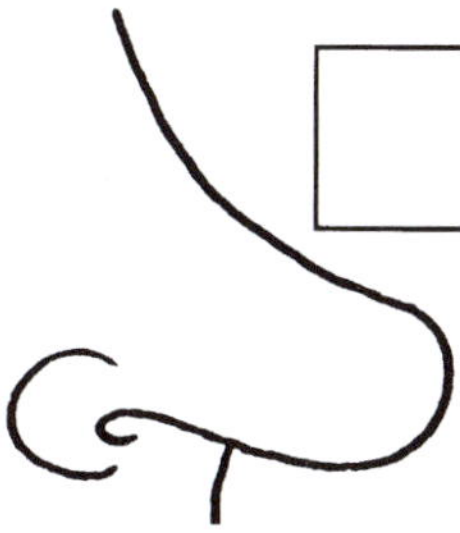

The letters r, n, and m

Write the letters and say the sounds.

r r r r r ➡ **r**ing

n n n n n ➡ **n**ose

m m m m m ➡ **m**ouse

Write the first sound in each box.
Colour the mug and net red.

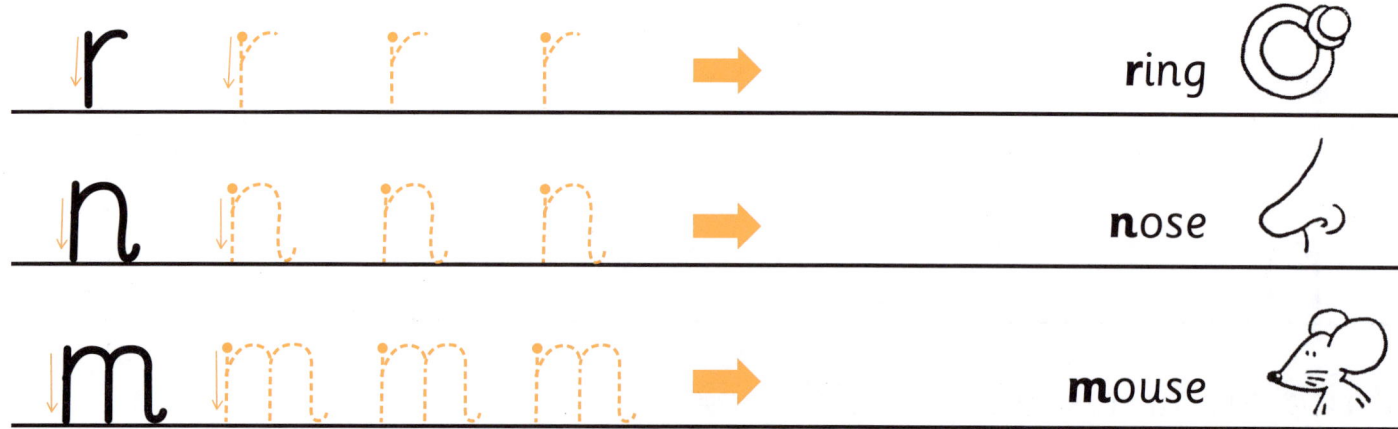

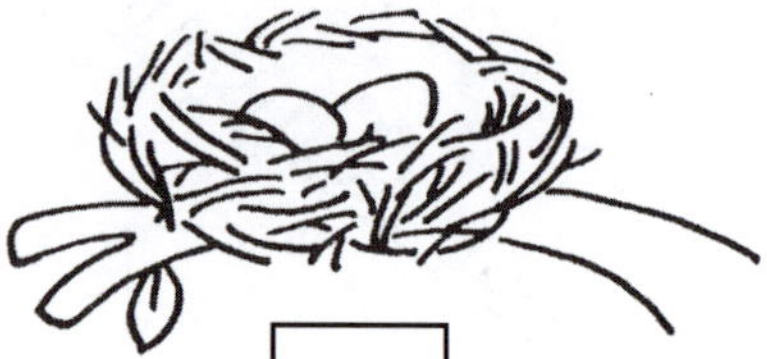

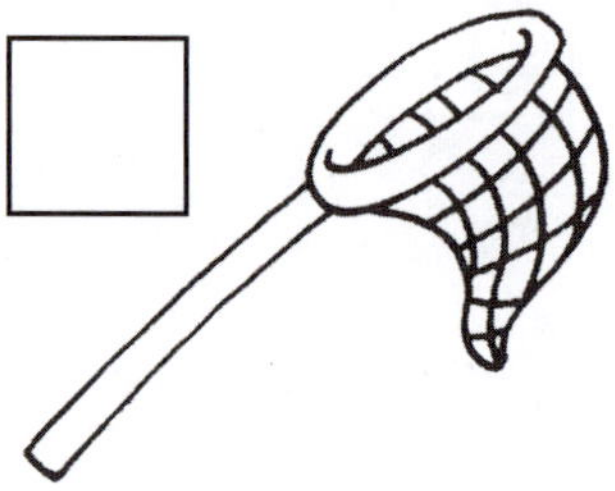

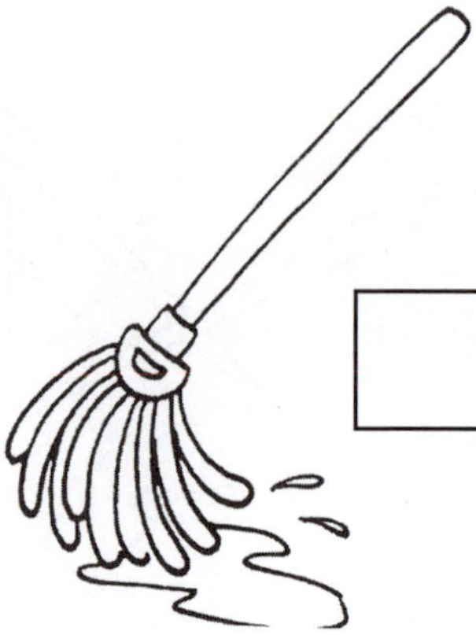

The letters h and m

Write the letters and say the sounds.

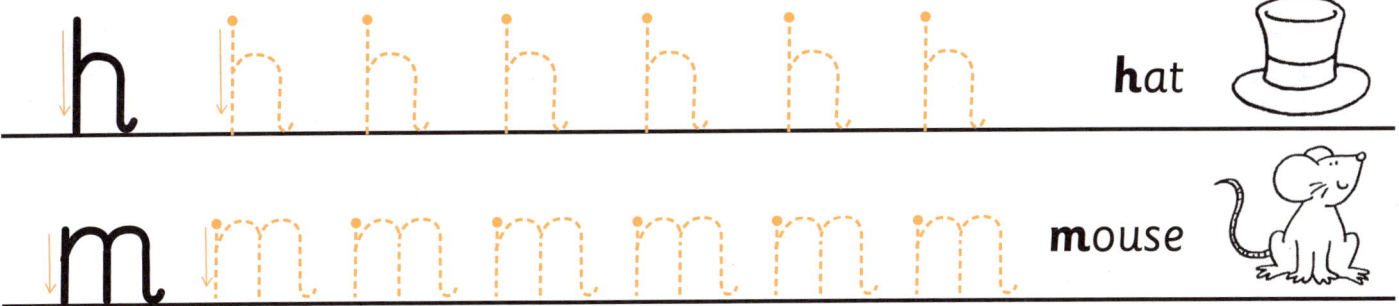

h h h h h h h h   **h**at

m m m m m m m m   **m**ouse

Write the first sound in each box.

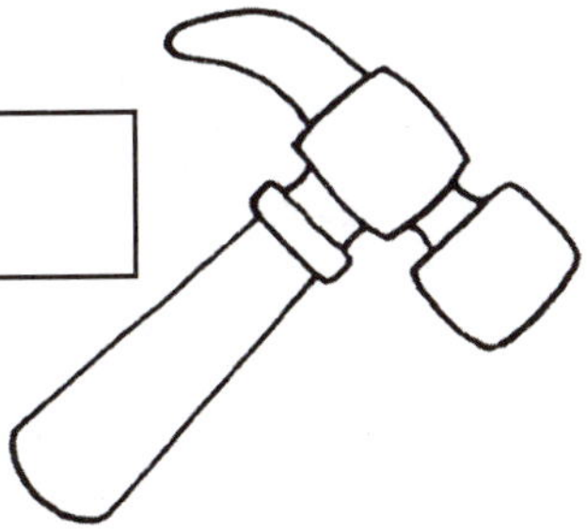

The letter p

Write the letter **p** and say the sound.

p p p p p p **p**encil

Write the first sound in each box.
Colour the birds.

The letters p and b

Write the letters and say the sounds.

b b b b b **b**ed

p p p p p **p**arrot

Write the first sound in each box.
Colour the fruit.

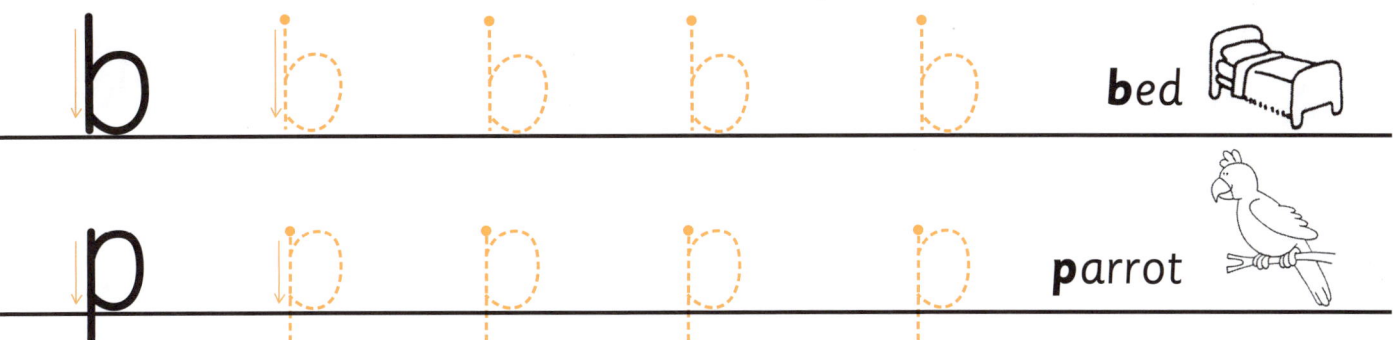

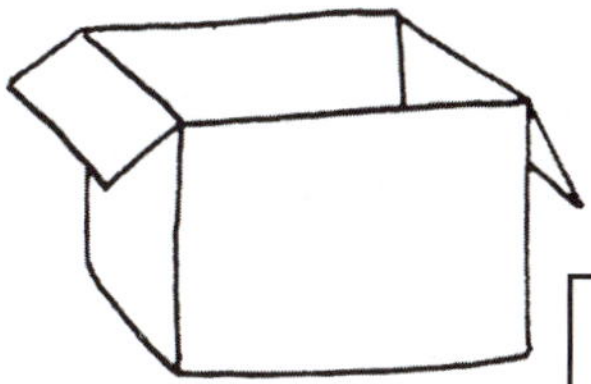

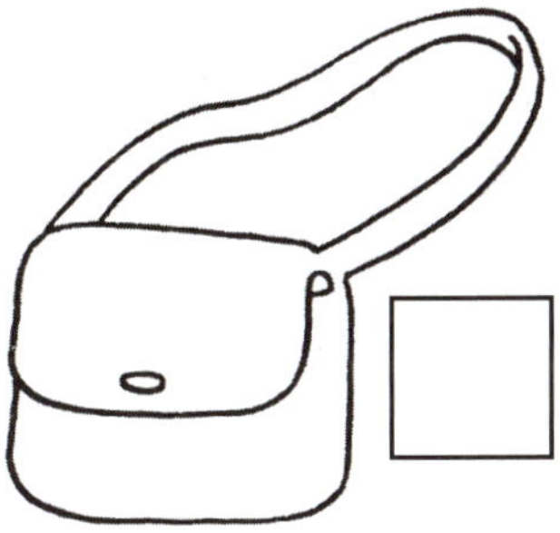

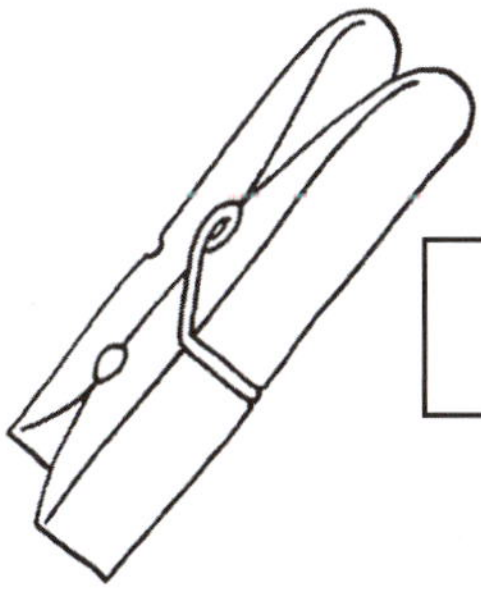

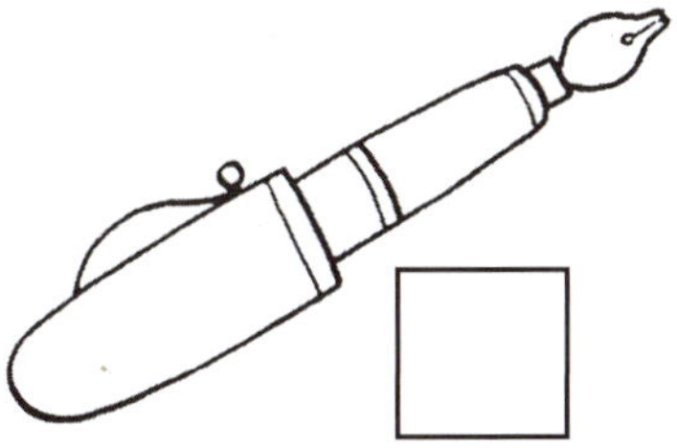

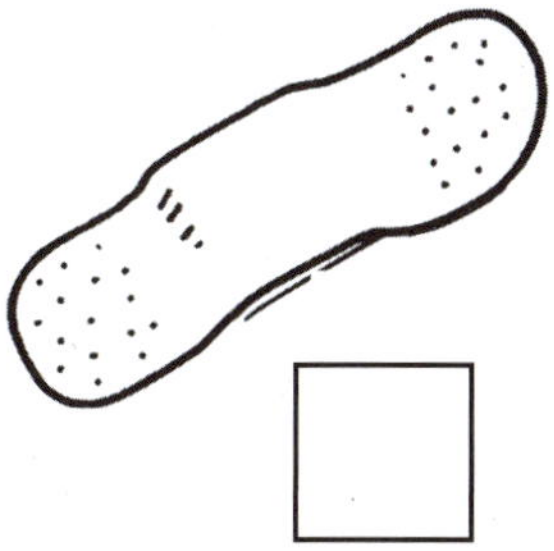

The letters l and t

Write the letters and say the sounds.

l l l l l l l l   **l**eg

t t t t t t t t   **t**orch

Write the first sound in each box.
Colour all the animals.

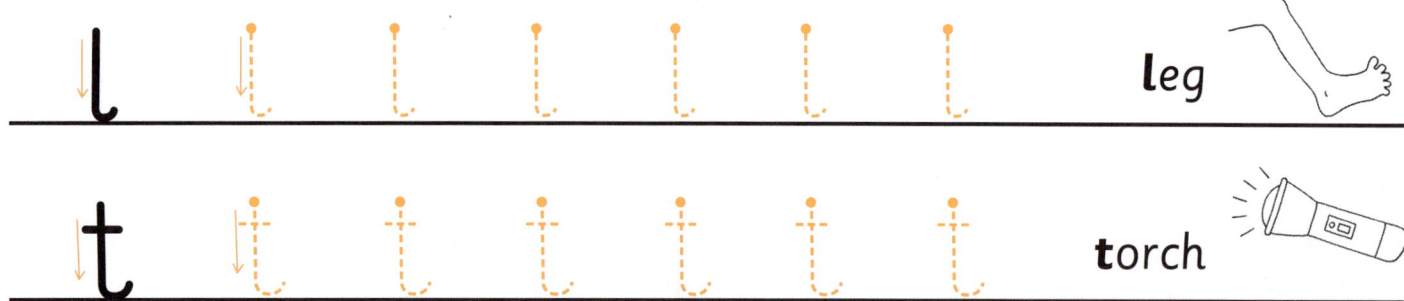

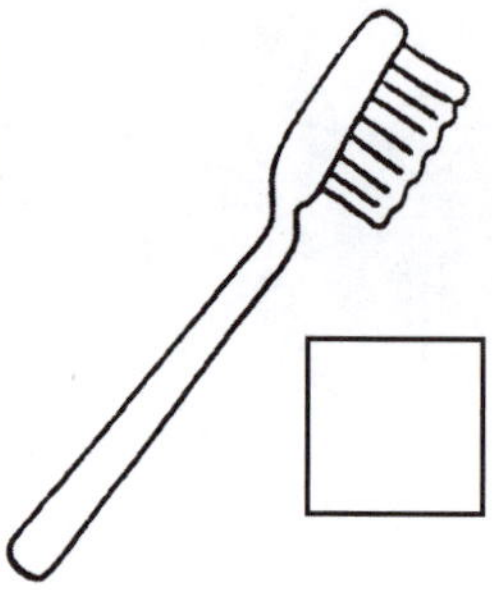

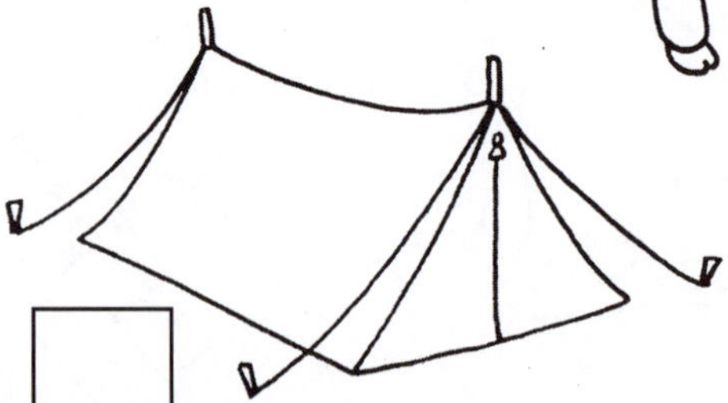

The letters l and t

Write the letters and say the sounds.

l l l l l l l l   **l**etter

t t t t t t t t   **t**eddy

Write the first sound in each box.
Colour ten pictures.

The letters j, u, and y

Write the letters and say the sounds.

j j j j   **j**ug

u u u u   **u**mbrella

y y y y   **y**acht

Write the first sound in each box.
Colour the yacht yellow.

The letters v and w

Write the letters and say the sounds.

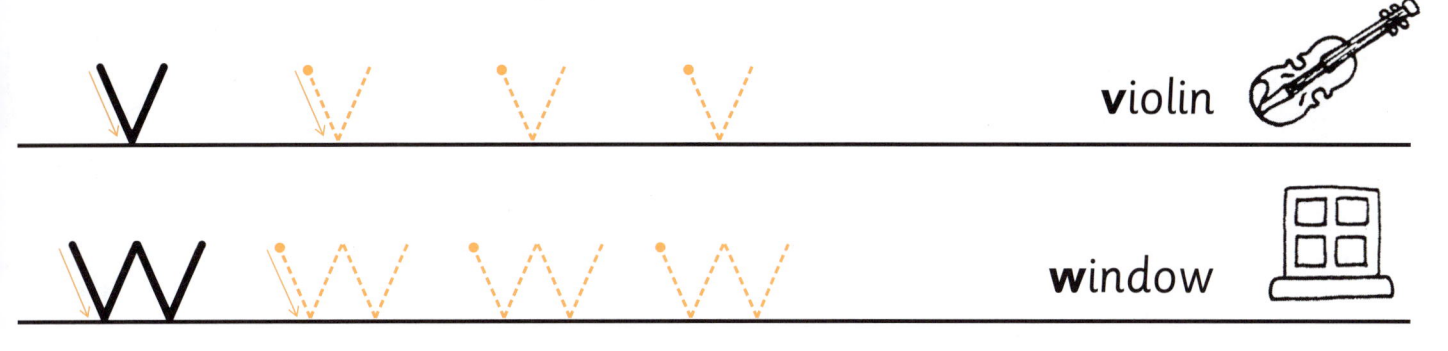

V v v v   **v**iolin

W w w w   **w**indow

Write the first sound in each box.
Colour the things that move.

The letter f

Write the letter and say the sound.

f f f f f f f f f   fish

f f f f f f f f f   flower

Write the first sound in each box.
Colour five pictures.

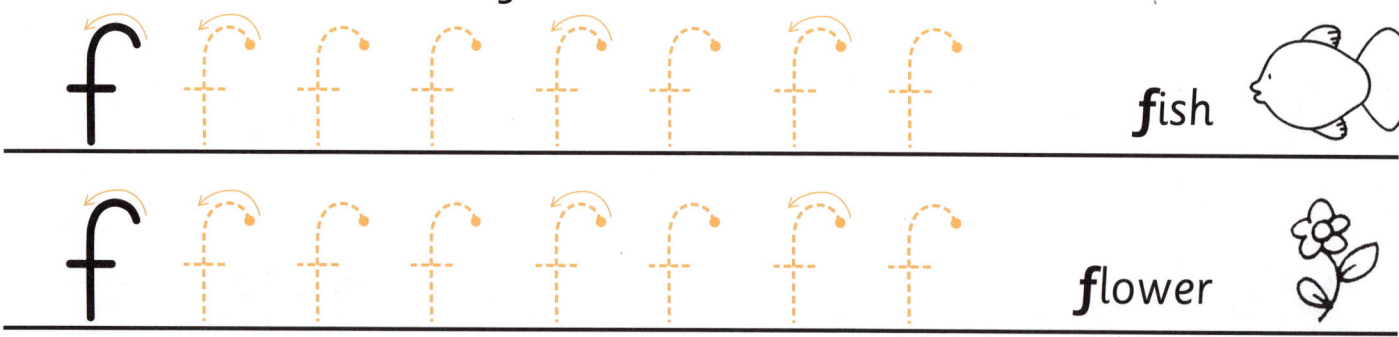

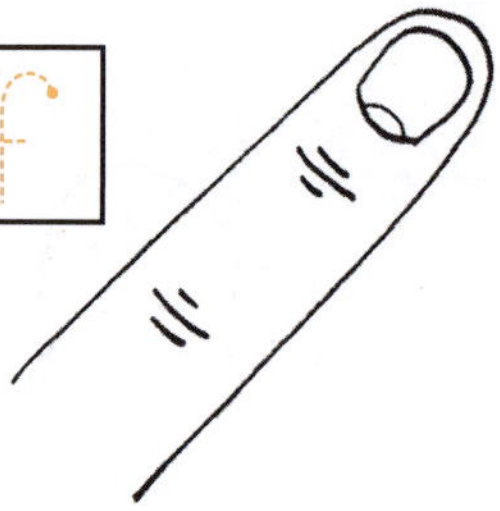

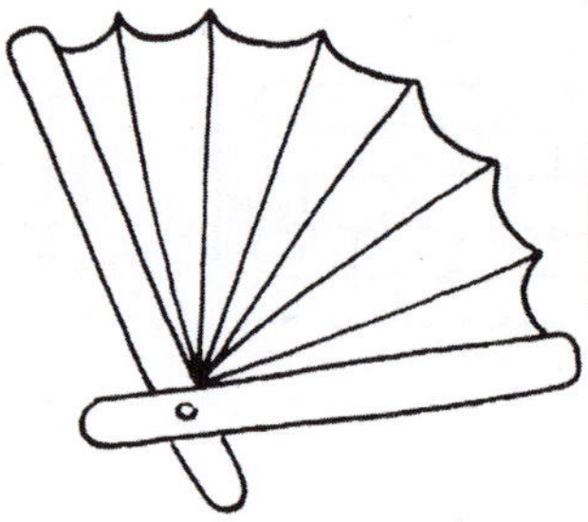

The letter k

Write the letter and say the sound.

k k k k k k k k

kite

Write the first sound in each box.

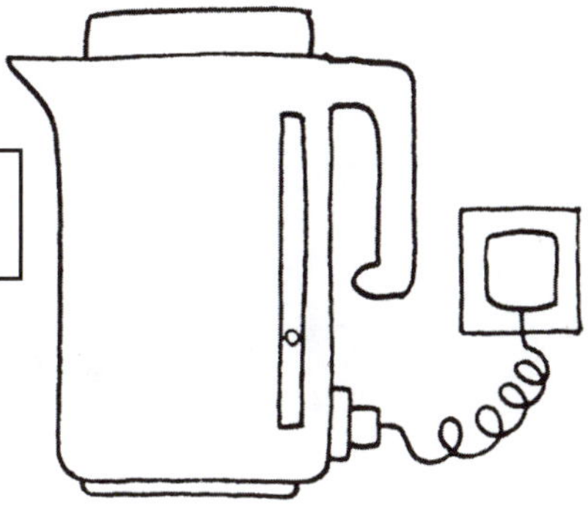

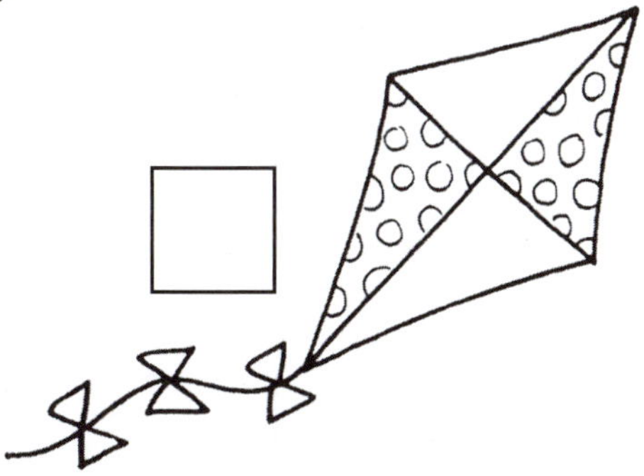

The alphabet

Say or sing the alphabet.
Write the letters and say the sounds.

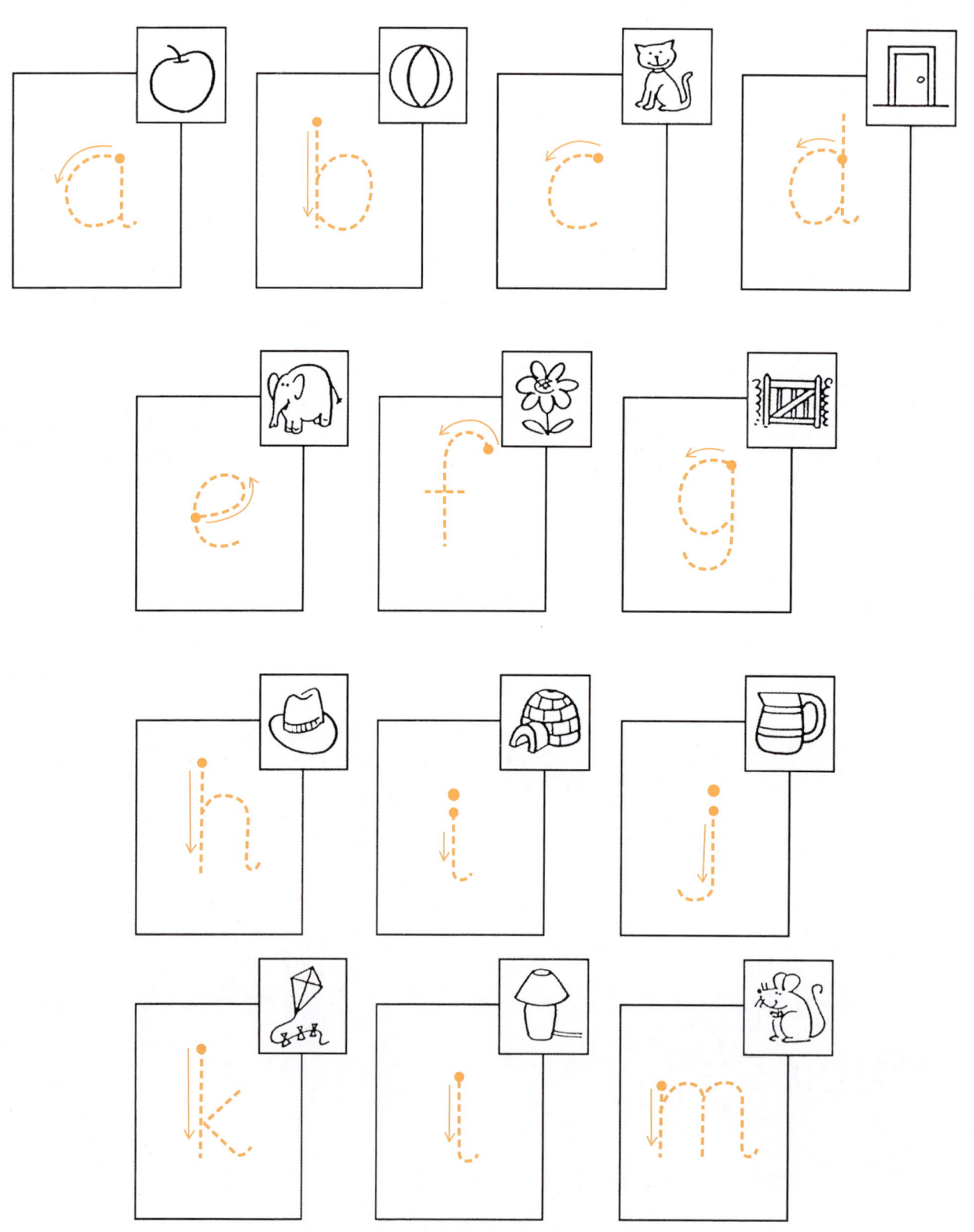

Summary of skills

Title	Page	Summary of skills
Drawing circles	4	Pencil control – drawing circles
Straight and curved lines	5	Pencil control – drawing different lines
Circles and lines	6	Pencil control – drawing circles and lines
The letters c and o	7	Name, sound and formation of letters
The letter a	8	Name, sound and formation of a letter
The letters o, a, and d	9	Name, sound and formation of letters
The letters c, g, and d	10	Name, sound and formation of letters
The letter s	11	Name, sound and formation of a letter
The letters c, a, d, and s	12	Name, sound and formation of letters
The letter e	13	Name, sound and formation of a letter
The letter e	14	Name, sound and formation of a letter
Vowels: a, e, i, o, u	15	Name, sound and formation of vowels
Vowels: a, e, i, o, u	16	Name, sound and identification of vowels
Vowels: a, e, i, o, u	17	Name, sound and formation of vowels
On or under?	18	Understanding prepositions and formation of letters
The letters r and n	19	Name, sound and formation of letters
The letters r, n, and m	20	Name, sound and formation of letters
The letters h and m	21	Name, sound and formation of letters
The letter p	22	Name, sound and formation of a letter
The letters p and b	23	Name, sound and formation of letters
The letters l and t	24	Name, sound and formation of letters
The letters l and t	25	Name, sound and formation of letters
The letters j, u, and y	26	Name, sound and formation of letters
The letters v and w	27	Name, sound and formation of letters
The letter f	28	Name, sound and formation of a letter
The letter k	29	Name, sound and formation of a letter
The alphabet	30	Saying and writing the alphabet
The alphabet	31	Saying and writing the alphabet

At Home With 3–5 years
abc	Reading
Colours	Shape & Size
Counting	Sounds & Rhymes
Letter Forms	Pattern & Shape
Numbers	Writing

At Home With 5–7 years
English	Phonics
French	Spelling 1
Handwriting 1	Spelling 2
Handwriting 2	Times Tables
Maths	

At Home With 7–9 years
English	Punctuation
French	Reasoning Skills – Verbal
Grammar	Reasoning Skills – Non Verbal
Maths	Spanish
Mental Maths	